Postcards from

by Katy Nayl

abuddhapress@yahoo.com

ISBN: 9798494603678

®™©

Cover art by @stuartmbuck

To Dave, who sees me through the apocalypse every day.

Contents

Baldr

Baldr

was the most beloved

of the gods

One night he saw

his own death

in a dream

Freyja, his mother

begged each creature

plant and rock

to swear an oath

to protect him

All agreed, happily

not to harm

this child of light

save one

The soft-leafed mistletoe

did not swear

so young

he had escaped

Freyja's notice

Baldr was immune

to all injury

the gods laughed

aimed missiles

for sport

hit their mark

Loki

jealous or just

lusting

for mischief

discovered the weakness

- mistletoe!-

fashioned a dart

Tricked blind Hothr

into aiming

it struck

deadly

through Baldr's heart

There was

one

final chance

if all would weep

for Baldr

he could return

from the land of the dead

Every man

each beast and plant

rock and metal

ran with sorrow

But Loki

refused to give

his tears

Baldr's fate

was sealed

and so began

the end of the world

We too

know the power

of mistletoe

the dart shot blind

the soft leaf

deceiving

The wound opens

our words turn to ash

and still

we will not weep

Guthrun

Many centuries ago

Guthrun, daughter of Gjuki

was married to King Atli against her will

her brothers slain

she waited years long for revenge

butchered her sons and served them to their father

and walked away, finally free

flames from the hall staining the sky behind her

Imagine nursing

such pain

such quiet purpose

that you'd gladly turn on your own future

toss the brand that sets your roof alight

Monday, 7:59am

leaves blow across the platform

the air is bitter, my coffee's growing cold

one more minute

one step forward

and I could bring these tired gables crackling down onto my head

Listen, you can hear it coming

you can already smell the smoke

Midgard

Week after weary week we walked

surviving on Kendal mint cake and scraps of conversation

waterproofs and shopping lists and late night wine and texts

our armour

until one day we realized

that the horizon we thought we'd been travelling towards

is in fact a serpent

biting its own tail

forever

and much, much closer than we think

Nastrands

There is a hall

that stands far from the sun

Its doors face north

its walls are made from woven snakes

bodies knotted

heads turned inwards

they spit rivers of poison

A cold wind

through the kitchen window

I focus on each breath

as the edge in your voice

begins to sharpen

and the tiled floor under my feet

begins to lurch

I'd steady myself

but I know my hand will rest on

scales

where the bricks should be

Sleipnir

Sleipnir was the best of horses.

His mother was Loki, who had turned himself into a mare for a single night.

***

Sleipnir carried the gods through the places where sea and sky meet, across the barriers between worlds.

***

At dusk I will walk along the beach and I will imagine that I am no longer confined by sea or shore or earth or sky or smoke or father or mother.

***

I will feel my eight hooves thundering through the sand and the salt and the spray and the clouds in my mane.

***

I will know the joyful passage from sphere to sphere and back

again, how sweet it is to fly across all bounds.

***

To go to hell and know that I was just passing through.

Thor

For you I would, joyfully

comb out my mighty beard

ride my goat-drawn chariot

make the sky resound with thunder

For you I would, joyfully

slay giants

devour herds

drain the sea in a single gulp

For you I would joyfully

stride across the hall

outsized, blundering

how I can make you laugh

For you I would, joyfully

battle the ice

the evening shadow creeping around my cup

paint a smile on my face

For you I would, joyfully

wrestle the serpent

that circles the earth

though you and I both know it will destroy me

Kraken

Danger is curled in small beginnings

The lock of hair that sparked the feud
the first soft sprig of mistletoe

The first disturbance in the water
before the splintering prow and the torn sail
the spear and shield dashed into the waves

It's hard to unravel the thread
trace ourselves back to the first papercut
the first white lie, the first joke that turned sour

By the time we noticed the ripples
we were already in its grip
and a great eye had blotted out the sun

Fenrir

I

It is said that at the end of all things, a wolf will swallow the sun.

No-one knows exactly when this will happen. The story goes that at the appointed time, the wolf will finally break the chains that have kept its jaws bound shut, and fulfil its destiny.

II

It's like sitting at the bottom of a swimming pool. Light and sound distant and distorted.

My lungs scream for air and I long to break for the surface.

I think about the weight of the water. I am heavy as a lead idol, when it should be the easiest thing in the world to float.

III

It gets dark earlier and earlier these days. A shadow that presses down into the corners of the kitchen and gouges deep tracks across the living room floor.

It would only take a single spark to lift the gloom, but for that I'd have to find a match. Maybe I'll sit here a while longer.

Outside my window I can hear breathing and the soft scrape of metal, link on link.

Idavoll

After Ragnarok

nothing but the sea shall remain

There will be silence

until

as slow as the dawn

on a winter's morning

the earth will come up from the waters

Vidar and Vali

Modi and Magni

children of the old gods

shall return to Idavoll

where their parents' home once stood

blind Hothr and Baldr will join them

released from the land of the dead

They will sit together

reminisce

about things past:

how the world ended

how a serpent encircled the earth

how the sun disappeared

into the jaws of a wolf

They will find the gilded chess pieces

scattered by their parents

My dream

is that one day

we too will sit on some far verandah

talk about old times

gather the fragments

that lie gleaming in the grass

as the earth gently rises

golden in the twilight

Yggdrasil

There are trees

that reach between worlds

these roots that connect us

Yggdrasil

Odin swings

half blind, drunk on wisdom

this trunk that connects us

casting wide swift ravens

Thought and Memory

these boughs that connects us

I lie awake

time stretched

ink-deep silence

these branches that connect us

soft rattle at the window

I reach across

a fretful canyon

this crown that connects us

soothed by the touch of feathers

I settle, warm in your hand

dreaming of water

these leaves that connect us

my breath

hour by hour

my life inscribed in a book

Acknowledgements

My thanks go to:

Red, for believing in this strange little collection, and for making the process of bringing it into the world so painless.

Not Deer Magazine, for publishing *Ygdrassil*

Expat Lit, for publishing *Fenrir*

Cypress Press, for including *Midgard* and *Nastrands* in their speculative poetry collection, *The Red House, Volume 2*

Craig, Judith, Verity and Vicky, for being my long-suffering beta readers, and unfailing sources of guidance and encouragement.

Dave, for listening to my ideas at 2am, and much more besides.

Manufactured by Amazon.ca
Bolton, ON